the global village

TRAVEL AND TOURISM

Carol Inskipp

Contents

Introduction

Tourism is one of the world's fastest-growing industries. International travel has never been easier. Today, people in more economically developed countries (MEDCs) can find out about vacations all over the world and book them at home using the Internet, as well as through travel agents. Television and other media have stimulated interest in other parts of the world by showing attractive and exciting images of far-away places. Improvements in air travel, especially the arrival of jumbo jets, have reduced the costs of long-distance travel.

Once only the rich could travel abroad, but now many people in industrialized countries can afford foreign vacations. They have enough leisure time and enough money to enjoy it. In contrast, however, most people in less economically developed countries (LEDCs) can rarely afford to take vacations, even within their own countries. Even people from some MEDCs choose not to travel abroad much. Only about 20 percent of Americans have passports, for example. They mainly take vacations in their own country.

What Is Tourism?

Tourism is travel mainly for recreation or leisure, and it accounts for about 75 percent of all international travel. What we call tourism covers a huge range of activities, from visits to friends within one's own country to international journeys, large-scale package tours abroad and family vacations organized by individuals. Along with trade and communications, travel is one of the

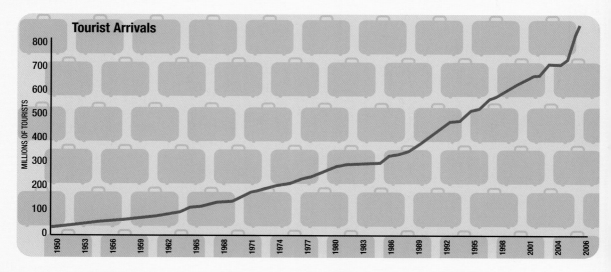

Tourist Arrivals

MILLIONS OF TOURISTS

800 — 700 — 600 — 500 — 400 — 300 — 200 — 100 — 0

1950 1953 1956 1959 1962 1965 1968 1971 1974 1977 1980 1983 1986 1989 1992 1995 1998 2001 2004 2006

▲ The growth of tourism is staggering. In 2006, another record year for tourism, there were 842 million international tourist arrivals.

▲ Tourism often spoils the very attractions visitors come to enjoy, as when too many people crowd onto a beach for their "place in the sun," for example.

largest areas of globalization—the growth of something on a worldwide scale.

Trends in tourism are changing. Some people want to stay in high-quality hotels in quiet resorts instead of having the traditional "sun, sea, and sand" package beach vacation. Adventure tourism—vacations for those with special interests, such as trekking or extreme sports—is a growing market.

Some tourist destinations have lost popularity because of too much vacation development, such as hotels and roads—Spain's Costa Brava is an example. Other countries are being visited much more than in the past because of peace after periods of war. These include countries such as Vietnam.

What Are the Benefits of Globalization?

Tourism is vital to the economies of many countries. LEDCs, especially, are increasingly turning to tourism to boost national earnings and create jobs. As much as 40 percent of the global services industry, providing accommodation, guiding, transportation and restaurants—is accounted for by tourism.

It can encourage pride in local traditions and support of local arts and crafts.

What Problems Has It Caused?

Tourism has grown rapidly and without being properly organized. This means that it has become a problem in industrialized countries and even more so in developing countries. It often harms local communities. Traditional cultures and ways of life are being lost. It is damaging the environment through pollution and overuse of resources. How can we strike a balance and increase the benefits of tourism, while also guarding against the risks?

Focus on...
Air Travel

International travel is more common in Europe than in the U.S. An explosion in low-cost air travel has contributed to a dramatic growth in foreign vacations. The number of budget airline flights has more than doubled in the past five years. In Europe, the low-cost airlines mainly operate from regional airports, which makes air travel more convenient for people who don't live in or near major cities.

Economic Impacts of Tourism

Tourism is the world's largest industry—bigger than cars, agriculture, or electronics. Spending on tourism worldwide was $800 billion in 2005 and is expected to more than double by 2020. The industry has large economic benefits in countries that tourists visit, especially foreign-exchange earnings. This is the money a country earns by selling things to other countries. Tourism is the main source of foreign-exchange earnings for 38 percent of all countries worldwide. Many poorer countries that have few natural resources, such as Madagascar, are unable to find other sources of foreign-exchange earnings.

Hidden Costs

There are many hidden costs to tourism. Often, rich countries are better able to profit from the industry than poor ones. Although the poorest countries have the most urgent need for money from tourism, they are the least able to benefit. Among the reasons for this is the large-scale transfer of money from tourism out of the country that is being visited. Local businesses

▼ Tourism is highly important to the economy of Gambia, one of the world's poorest countries. As many as 30 percent of workers depend directly or indirectly on tourism.

and products are mainly cut out, too. In most package tours, where almost all costs are included, nearly 90 percent of the money spent by tourists goes to international companies, rather than local businesses or workers. This is known as leakage. A recent study of tourism leakage in Thailand estimated that the vast majority of all money spent by tourists ended up leaving the country via foreign-owned tour operators, airlines, hotels, imported drinks, and food.

Effects on Local Economies

Increasing demands for services and goods from tourists often cause high price rises for local people, whose income does not increase to cover the costs. A recent study in Belize found that prices for goods had increased by eight percent because of tourism. The value of land and costs of buildings may rise so much that locals can no longer buy them. This can lead to richer people from overseas moving in and economic opportunities being lost for local residents. In Costa Rica, about 65 percent of hotels belong to foreigners.

The demands of tourism can make local governments improve water and sewage systems, roads, and supplies of electricity, which benefits local communities. However, these developments can cost local governments and taxpayers a great deal of money that they cannot afford.

Failures in the economy in a country can be devastating for tourism, like the crisis that hit parts of Asia in 1997. This financial disaster led to a sharp fall in tourist numbers arriving in Thailand, Malaysia, and Indonesia in 1997 and 1998.

Focus on...
Leakage

Of each $100 spent on a vacation by a tourist from an MEDC, only $5 actually stays in an LEDC's economy. This is partly because tourists demand food and other products that the host country cannot supply. Large foreign businesses often have a big share in tourism, as they are the only ones with enough money to pay for the basic organization of tourism, such as hotels, restaurants, and other services. The profits they make generally go straight back to their own countries.

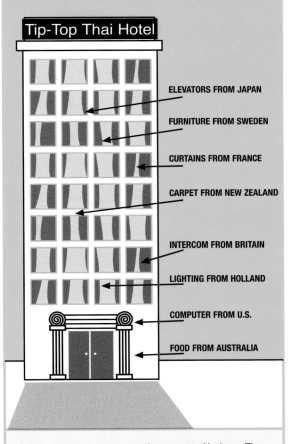

Tip-Top Thai Hotel

ELEVATORS FROM JAPAN

FURNITURE FROM SWEDEN

CURTAINS FROM FRANCE

CARPET FROM NEW ZEALAND

INTERCOM FROM BRITAIN

LIGHTING FROM HOLLAND

COMPUTER FROM U.S.

FOOD FROM AUSTRALIA

▲ This diagram demonstrates the concept of leakage. The facilities in a hotel are provided by wealthier nations, and the hotel itself will be owned by one. A large percentage of the profits earned go back to these wealthy countries, and very little remains in the country in which the hotel is located.

▲ Traditional handicrafts, such as these woven cloths made by women in Bhutan, are sold to tourists. Such crafts are vital to the tourist economy of the country.

Employment Opportunities

Tourism has created millions of jobs in global and local businesses—2.5 million jobs in 2006 alone. People work in hotels, restaurants, taxi services, and souvenir sales. Many are also employed indirectly through the supply of goods and services to tourism-related businesses, such as bakers who produce bread for tourists staying in hotels.

Although tourism provides one in 10 jobs around the world, these jobs are usually unskilled, poorly paid, and of low status. Often, jobs are seasonal, and there is no guarantee of employment from one year to the next. Workers frequently move in from elsewhere for these jobs. Other problems facing employees are difficulties in getting training. Their experience may not be recognized as important. Tourist workers may also face poor housing conditions.

Improvements for Local Businesses

Tourism often contributes to local economies, especially as the large majority of tourism jobs are in small or medium-sized firms. Money earned from tourism is important for local guides, rickshaw owners, boatmen, and people selling from street stalls.

Making handicrafts at home for tourists enables women and native communities, especially the poor, to earn valuable income, which they would not be able to do otherwise. Weaving by women throughout the small Himalayan kingdom of Bhutan, one of the world's poorest countries, produces cloth with distinctive patterns and bright colors from vegetable dyes. The woven cloth is vital to Bhutan's culture, especially as the people always wear traditional dress.

Eyewitness

"Today, the travel and tourism economy is responsible for over 230 million jobs and more than 10 percent of the gross domestic product worldwide. As new models for travel and tourism develop, more and more tourist destinations are seeking advice from us on achieving healthy economies that are sustainable in the long term."
World Travel and Tourism Council

▲ The devastation caused by the Asian tsunami in 2004 led to a dramatic drop in tourist numbers in all the affected areas.

Now, weaved cloth handicrafts have become popular with tourists.

Changing Values

Tourism can upset local economies and change cultural values, resulting in links among society becoming weaker and eventually contributing to the breakdown of communities. In Bali, for example, tour guides and drivers can earn $400–500 a month, compared with a monthly salary of just $100–150 earned by a teacher who is far better trained.

Some countries are at risk because they have become too dependent on tourism as a main source of income. This can be damaging if a political or environmental disaster keeps tourists away. In December 2004, the Maldives were hit by tsunamis, a series of giant ocean waves. The islands' tourism industry—which supports 83 percent of the country's workers directly or indirectly—was badly affected. In 2002, more than 200 people were killed by bombings in a tourist district on Bali. Bali was the chief tourist destination in Indonesia, and tourism contributed at least half of the island's economy. A month after the attack, tourist arrivals dropped by nearly 60 percent, although they gradually increased to former levels within two years. Even a small disturbance—a kidnapping, fire, local disease outbreak, or political protest—can reduce bookings.

Have Your Say

People in many LEDCs depend on the money they earn from the tourist industry to support their families, but it can be a mixed blessing.

• What long-term effects might there be in LEDCs if unqualified workers in the tourist industry end up being better paid than professionals?
• Should visitors support local economies by buying souvenirs that have been made locally, or is it unfair to ask people to spend money on products they do not really want?

11

▲ Trekking is very hard work for porters, who have to carry heavy loads. A recent survey found that nearly half of Nepalese porters have had medical problems on treks.

Working Conditions

Many jobs in tourism are low paid. This is true in both MEDCs, such as the United States, and LEDCs. According to a 2002 study, a tourism industry worker in Missouri, if employed full-time, made nearly 37 percent less per year than the average worker in the state. In addition, many tourism industry jobs were seasonal or part-time.

Porters who carry supplies for tourists on trekking vacations can experience particularly poor working conditions. Tourism in Nepal—a country in the central Himalayas—relies heavily on income from trekking. However, porters earn very small wages, usually only $4–6 a day. Most of them are employed on a casual basis. Some die every year due to the

effects of high altitude. Frequently, they have poor footwear, such as old sneakers or even flip-flops, and not enough warm clothes or sleeping bags.

The International Porter Protection Group (IPPG) and Tourism Concern (a UK-based pressure group) campaign for better conditions for porters. They educate trekking tourists and ask governments for help. They have also built shelters for porters, and encourage travel agencies to consider porter safety through a code of ethics. Trekking tourism provides vital income for mountain communities. Tourists can help by making sure they use a travel agent that has made a commitment to protecting its porters.

Women and Children

In LEDCs in particular, women and children can suffer as a result of their employment in the tourism industry. The International Labor Organization estimates that as many as 13–19 million young people under the age of 18 work in tourism. This is 10–15 percent of the global tourism labor force. According to the United Nations, one million children are sexually abused by tourists every year.

Women make up around 70 percent of the labor force in tourism. Most women are employed in jobs that are similar to traditional domestic roles. They are chiefly employed as cleaners, babysitters, waitresses, receptionists, and travel-agency sales people. Relatively few are in jobs where they make important decisions or are involved in planning. They are even more likely to have casual or part-time work, and generally have fewer training opportunities than male workers in tourism. The United Nations has recommended that employers set up programs that give women training and appoint them to more responsible jobs, such as managers.

▼ The economic benefits of tourism clearly lie in MEDCs, with the United States topping the chart for tourist income.

International Tourism Receipts (2005)

Rank		$ billion
1	United States	81.7
2	Spain	47.9
3	France	42.3
4	Italy	35.4
5	United Kingdom	30.7
6	China	29.3
7	Germany	29.2
8	Turkey	18.2
9	Austria	15.5
10	Australia	15.0

(Data as collected by UNWTO, 2006)

Eyewitness

Anna works as a housekeeper at a large hotel in the Dominican Republic. She works a nine-hour day and cleans 21 rooms. Anna is widowed with two children. She does not get paid for vacation, or for the long overtime hours she has to work. She would like a union to give her more security, but the hotel will not allow it.

"The conditions for the worker in the Dominican Republic are very poor. We live thinking every day what we're going to eat. We have to go to work every day thinking of this. We have to smile to the tourists, but it is not what we are feeling in our hearts. We want to work and we want to make holidays [vacations] happy for tourists, but it is difficult when we are so badly treated."
Tourism Concern

▼ A young girl sells postcards to tourists on the streets in Myanmar. Often, people in LEDCs have to rely on a small income from the tourism industry just to earn enough to survive.

Cultural Impacts of Tourism

Some people point out that an important benefit of tourism is that it enables people to gain a first-hand knowledge from cultures and traditions very different from their own. Experiencing other cultures encourages a greater understanding and tolerance of different people's beliefs and ideals. Others say the sharp contrast between the wealth of tourists and the poverty of the host countries is a major negative influence that tourism has brought to LEDCs.

Positive Impacts

Tourism can result in the peaceful coming together of people from different countries, cultures, and occupations. Understanding, friendship, and respect can all develop as people from different cultures get to know one another better. Tourists can have fun in ways that respect the cultures and lifestyles of the people living in the countries they are visiting. The customs and way of life in the host country are more likely to be preserved because visitors value them.

Some cultural events have been created specifically for tourists, while also bringing huge benefits to local people—the Edinburgh International Festival in Scotland, for example. This festival presents a rich program of classical music, theater, opera, and dance in six major theaters and concert halls, as well as a number of smaller places for art and entertainment. Many thousands of people go to the festival and stay in Edinburgh, providing residents with valuable income every year. The festival promotes the people's pride in being Scottish and in their own country. It encourages Scottish traditions, as these are what visitors have come to Edinburgh to see.

Negative Impacts

The tourists' world of luxury accommodation, air-conditioned cars, and lavish restaurants while on vacation gives local people a false image of what the visitors' everyday lives are actually like at home. Local people who work in tourism can have their own opinion of themselves damaged, as they are forced to serve the visitors.

▲ The military tattoo outside Edinburgh Castle is the centerpiece of the month-long arts festival that takes place there every year.

▲ Locals put on a traditional dance show for tourists visiting Micronesia. While such performances can educate visitors, they often reduce the original meaning and importance of the ceremony.

Throughout LEDCs, traditional dances, music, and crafts that formed part of local people's cultural heritage have been specially prepared for tourists. Ancient ways of life are reduced to being exotic products that are advertised and sold. This often means changing a cultural experience to suit the tastes of visitors, until it bears little or no resemblance to the original. Dances and religious ceremonies often lose their deeper spiritual value and become meaningless. Local people are only valued for being photographed. This can be degrading and humiliating.

Loss of culture is not limited to LEDCs. For example, the phenomemon known as McDonaldization is dominating more and more aspects of lives in the industrialized world, especially in the United States.

McDonaldization is a word introduced to describe how society is becoming like a fast-food restaurant.

Focus on...
McDonaldization

McDonaldization means being efficient, but all is predictable and calculated to be exactly the same. For instance, McDonald's food outlets look the same everywhere in the world, and their hamburgers are identical in thickness, size, and contents. Some vacations are dominated by McDonaldization. Travel agencies transport middle-class Americans to 10 European capitals in just 14 days. Each visitor experiences exactly the same hotels, restaurants, and tourist sites. While such experiences of other civilizations and cultures have some value, no one has the opportunity to meet local people. The efficiency of the trip brings reduced prices, but this is at the cost of enjoyable and educational experiences.

Indigenous Peoples

Indigenous peoples and knowledge of their cultural heritage have become increasingly sought-after by the tourism industry. For many native people, tourism is often unwelcome, and is usually imposed on them without their having any say in how it is carried out, or without their agreement. Their cultures, sacred and religious sites, heritage, homes, beaches, and livelihoods have frequently been damaged. Often they have seen little economic benefit. The young are eager to leave their rural homes and traditions behind. Yet it is often these traditional lifestyles, arts, crafts, and culture that tourists have come to see.

Hawaii Religious Sites

The building of hotels and resorts is to blame for the destruction of some ancient Hawaiian sacred sites. In 1991, a burial ground was excavated to make way for a resort on the island of Kauai, for example. Protests by the local people led to just a very small part of the area being set aside for the remains.

Hill Tribes in Thailand

Less than a third of the million hill-tribe people in northern Thailand have legal rights to land or rights as citizens of the country, yet they are important for attracting tourists to the area—second only to trekking, according to the Tourism Authority of Thailand. Despite this, hardly any money is invested back into the region; only tour operators and a few middlemen profit. Tourists tend to treat hill tribes as some kind of exotic beings, taking photos and giving chocolate to the children.

▲ A Thai hill-tribe woman in traditional dress. Some tourists come to see the local people not to discover more about their culture, but to look at them as though they were exhibits in a museum.

Kankanaeys in Philippines

The Kankanaeys are the original people of Sagada Province, a Philippine destination popular with tourists because of its distinctive mountain-village atmosphere. A recent dramatic increase in tourist numbers is now threatening the Kankanaeys' way of life. Traditional customs, which honor their land and the passage of time, are being spoiled by over-curious tourists who show no respect. Tourists have even written graffiti on the walls of sacred burial caves and wooden coffins, and taken bones of the natives' ancestors as souvenirs.

Tourist Behavior

Tourists can cause offense easily—perhaps without realizing it—just because they are unaware of acceptable behavior in the country they are visiting. For example, Tibetan Buddhists consider it offensive to walk past a prayer wall on the right instead of the left side. In many Asian and African countries, women wearing shorts and bare-chested men are considered very rude. Women are expected to keep their heads covered when outdoors in some Muslim countries. At the sacred aboriginal site of Uluru in central Australia, many tourists ignore the aborigines' requests not to climb the rock because this would anger their ancestors, even though the requests are clearly stated on signs near the rock and at the information center.

Eyewitness

Dawa Tenzing belongs to the Sherpas, a mountain tribe who live in the high Himalayas in Nepal near Mt. Everest, the world's highest peak. After half a century of assisting expeditions to climb Everest, and watching tens of thousands of trekkers file past his home at a remote monastery near the mountain, Dawa made this comment:

"Many people come, looking, looking, taking picture. Too many people. No good… Some people, come, see. Good!"

Dawa meant that many visitors who walk past his monastery look and take photos, but only some of them really try to understand and value what they are seeing.

▼ Uluru has a great spiritual significance for Australian aboriginals. They believe that climbing the rock and taking photographs of certain parts of it disturbs their ancestors, but many tourists do not respect these beliefs.

Displacement of Peoples

Local communities are sometimes forced off their land, or people are turned out from their homes, to make way for tourist development. Families and communities can be evicted without warning, compensation, or being given somewhere else to live.

Bedul Bedouin

The Bedul Bedouin tribe lives around Petra, the best-known archeological site and most popular tourism attraction in Jordan, set in a spectacular desert environment. The Bedul lived in ancient caves at the site and worked as poor farmers with small plots of land and herds of goats. In the 1980s, when a plan was developed to create a national park at Petra, they were gradually persuaded to move out of their cave homes, although many did not want to leave and continued to live there until 1990.

The Bedul were moved to a village built for them on the edge of the park. The village has brought better health care and education, but it is overcrowded. The Bedul are not able to reach their old farming lands, and there is not enough land around their new village to support their farming. Many Bedul have had to give up farming and are now making money from tourism instead—the only choice they have. They sell drinks and cheap souvenirs to tourists and act as guides. But their traditional culture and way of life are fast disappearing. Tourism has also caused divisions amongst the Bedul. Some people have become wealthy by tribal standards, while many others remain poor.

▼ The caves at Petra in Jordan had been home to the Bedul Bedouin people. Today, they form part of a national park and are a popular tourist attraction.

▲ The majority of Maasai communities do not benefit from the tourism industry. They are not even employed in lodges and camps, because tour operators employ staff from other parts of the country.

Maasai in East Africa

The Maasai people live in Kenya and Tanzania, where they traditionally look after cattle, goats, and sheep, often moving with their herds to find fresh pastures. Since the 1960s, large areas of their land have been taken over for farms, wildlife parks, and tourism. The Maasai lost more than 1.5 million acres (.6 million ha) in Kenya between 1974 and 1998. Some of their homes were completely destroyed, and some livestock were rounded up and sold by the government. The Maasai received no compensation. Throughout East Africa, national parks and their wildlife are being conserved at the expense of the Maasai who used to live there.

Recently, some of the Maasai communities have started fighting back with their own tourism projects developed in partnership with responsible tourism businesses. One of these is African Initiatives, a social justice group that organizes treks in Tanzania.

Tourists can walk with and meet the Hadza hunter-gatherers for two weeks. They stay with a Maasai community, and during the trek, they visit the Serengeti plains and the World Heritage site of the magnificent Ngorongoro Crater, two of the best places to see wildlife in Africa.

Eyewitness

After being away for 10 years, Anna, a young lawyer working in London, returned to her home country of Jamaica for a vacation.

"I found that only tourists can use the best beaches, and it is no longer possible for local people to go there. Fishermen have suffered most, as they can no longer bring their boats onto the beaches and land their catches. All I wanted to do was walk along the sand, but a security guard stopped me. I wasn't even allowed to dip my toes in the water! Our beaches are lovely, but they should be enjoyed by everyone."

Adivasis

Tribal people in India are known as Adivasis, and they form 8.4 percent of the country's population—as many as 84 million people. Often, they have been forced to move from their traditional forest homes to make way for wildlife parks. This has resulted in long-lasting conflicts between park staff and local communities, such as those at Nagarahole in Karnataka.

Until about six years ago, Periyar Wildlife Reserve, Kerala's most-visited area set aside for the protection of wildlife, faced the same problems as most other protected areas in India. The relationship between the reserve staff and local people was very difficult. Large-scale smuggling of valuable sandalwood and the poaching of wild animals were common. Since then, officials at Periyar have managed to turn this situation around by helping the Adivasis earn money through tourism. In the late 1990s, reserve staff started talks with the Adivasis, offering to help solve their problems. Then the reserve staff contacted hotels and asked them to include forest treks in the tourist itinerary. Adivasis, who once were poachers and know the forest better than anyone else, now lead tourist treks through the reserve. The program is very successful. Now the Adivasis have an interest in conservation at Periyar, as they make more money from guiding than they did from killing wildlife illegally. Poaching has decreased, and the numbers of some mammals have noticeably increased.

Preservation of Sites

In many places, tourism has encouraged people to value their ancient sites and monuments more, and to restore and preserve

▲ The Great Wall of China is one of the best-known attractions in the world. Its fame has meant that parts visited by tourists have been restored and are protected.

them. People come to these well-developed and cared-for sites, but making these visits alone does not give a true picture of the country. For example, Cambodia is nothing like the area around Angkor Wat.

● Angkor Wat temple is the most important tourist attraction in Cambodia and has become a symbol of the country, appearing on its national flag. It was built in the early 12th century for King Suryavarman II as his state temple. Considerable work was carried out in the 20th century to remove vegetation and soil that had gathered on the ruins.

- The Mayans built impressive monuments in Guatemala between 700 B.C. and A.D. 900, to pay tribute to their past rulers. When rediscovered, the ruins were buried in a forest, and an enormous amount of work was needed to uncover them. Most ruins are at Tikal, which is one of Guatemala's top tourist attractions today. More than 3,000 monuments have been revealed there.

- The Great Wall of China was built and maintained between the fifth century B.C. and the sixteenth century A.D. to protect the northern borders of the Chinese empire. It is the world's longest man-made structure, stretching about 4,000 miles (6,352 km). Several walls have been built, the most famous by the first emperor of China, Qin Shi Huang, who conquered all opposing states and unified China in 221 B.C. Sections of the Great Wall near Beijing and near tourist sites have been protected and even rebuilt, but large sections of the wall elsewhere have been neglected.

- Sigirya was an ancient palace and fortress in Sri Lanka, built by King Kassapa I in the fifth century, on the summit of a granite peak. The upper palace on top of the rock has huge tanks cut into the rock that still hold water. Lovely paintings of dancing ladies once covered parts of the rock. Only a small number remain, but they are in wonderful condition.

Have Your Say

Small communities of native people have often suffered hardship by being removed from their homes and land to make way for tourist development or national parks, although the country as a whole has benefited from tourism.

- Is it right that communities are moved from their homes and land where they have lived and worked traditionally for many years?
- As the numbers of native people are small, should the interests of the whole country come first, and native people be given new homes and land close by?
- How might these communities maintain their culture, way of life, and self respect after they are forced to move away?

▲ The paintings and surviving ruins and moats at the Sri Lankan rock fortress of Sigirya are carefully preserved, and are admired by huge numbers of tourists every year.

Tourism and Natural Resources

Tourism uses up basic resources. Its demands for wood to use as fuel and for building lodges are contributing to forest destruction, especially in some LEDCs. Overuse of resources is also a problem in industrialized countries, such as Spain, where tourism has put a great strain on water resources.

Energy Use

Energy use by each tourist is often very high. Saving energy can reduce costs considerably, as well as cut emissions of carbon dioxide, a major cause of climate change. In New Zealand, a recent study found that transportation was the main source of energy use by tourists, making up as much as 69 percent of the energy used by international tourists within the country.

Large hotels can be highly wasteful of energy. Guests often show little concern for how much electricity and water they might consume. A recent U.S. study found that tourists in the country used large amounts of energy for air conditioning, laundry, elevators, drying, lighting, heating rooms and swimming pools, waste disposal, and transportation. In many cases, resorts did not bother to use natural features, such as wind for cooling, or sun for either heating or drying.

▼ Shuttle buses, like this one used by a hotel in Florida, can help the environment by limiting the number of private cars used by visitors.

▲ These solar panels at a popular tourist destination—the Sossusvlei sand dunes in Namibia—are part of a sustainable management program that also includes recycling and using local materials for building.

Energy-Efficient Tourism

The study also found that there are great possibilities for reducing energy use in the tourism industry. Large hotels have a greater potential to save energy than smaller ones, because they are often part of a chain, which generally has more money to spend than small companies. New hotels and resort developments can plan for energy efficiency and the use of renewable energy sources, such as wind and solar power, as they are being constructed. Existing hotels can make improvements by conducting an environmental check of current energy use. This will find out where and how savings can be made.

There are now about 20 ski areas in the United States that use renewable energy to generate their electricity. Resorts can provide guests with frequent bus shuttles and offer discounts or free parking for carpooling to reduce car use and energy used in transportation.

Reductions in energy use can often result in worthwhile savings in a very short time. A Seattle hotel overhauled its entire lighting system and cut its electricity bill from lighting by two-thirds. A Washington, D.C., resort has saved large amounts of energy by: not heating unoccupied rooms; changing bed linen every four days instead of every day; using compact fluorescent light bulbs, which are much more efficient than ordinary bulbs; having double-glazed windows; and using waste heat from the kitchen and laundry to heat water.

Focus on...
South Africa

A recent study found that:

- For every 10 percent increase in the room-temperature setting, energy costs rise by about 25 percent.
- Installing a solar water heater that heats water using energy from the sun can save 15–30 percent of electricity costs.
- Every 9°F (5°C) reduction in water temperature reduces the cost of washing by up to 13 percent.
- Insulating roofs and heating pipes can save up to 50 percent on heating bills.

▲ Vacationers expect swimming pools in hotels in hot countries, but such pools can place demands on limited water supplies in dry areas.

Water Use

According to the United Nations, the average tourist uses as much water in 24 hours as a villager in an LEDC would use to produce rice for 100 days. Goa, in southern India, is a popular tourist resort with a serious water shortage. Local women have to walk increasingly longer distances to fetch fresh water, as the booming tourism industry soaks it up for hotels.

Water shortages are also developing in parts of the U.S. as water demand exceeds supply. In some places, tourism is one of the causes of this, in particular on Hawaii and in many cities and towns in northern Arizona.

Problems in the Mediterranean

Increasing tourist levels in the Mediterranean are destroying valuable wetlands. Tourists also use some water supplies that local communities depend on. In summer, up to 225 gallons (850 l) of water per person per day can be used to meet tourist demands. This is almost four times the amount of water used daily by an average Spaniard living in a city. Water shortages are likely to cause more problems in summer, when tourism is at its highest level. Natural water supplies are least available then because of lower rainfall and higher temperatures.

Eyewitness

"We will restrict the use of water just to maintain our greens and our golfing fairways. Sometimes we water the greens by hand to reduce overspill. Maybe it's a little more labor intensive, but everyone benefits. I hope that money generated by the golf club will be plowed back into the economy."

Golf course chief executive, Barbados Golf Club. The club has an 18-hole course, which consumes hundreds of thousands of gallons of water a day, despite Barbadians often being asked to ration their own water use.

A tourist boom is expected over the next 20 years, and this will strain water resources further. Water-guzzling tourist attractions, such as water parks, golf courses, and swimming pools, continue to be built and could eventually dry up the very resource that they depend on. The World Wide Fund for Nature believes the amount of water tourists use in the Mediterranean region could be halved if water-saving ideas were acted upon, such as putting water-saving devices in tourist accommodations. Water that has been used for washing can be used again to water golf courses and lawns. Reducing water use would also save money by cutting the water bills of hotels.

Focus on...
The Boom in Vietnam

The problem of excessive water use is now being tackled by some tourism organizations. For example, Vietnam is in the middle of a tourism boom, and tourism development has greatly reduced fresh water supplies on Cat Ba Island. The U.S. Agency for International Development is supporting efforts to introduce environmentally friendly tourism actions that will bring financial benefits to local people. These include training hotel owners to meet standards for reduced water and electricity use.

▼ This golf course in the U.S. is being watered during a drought. It takes nearly half a million gallons (2 million l) of water a day to keep the grass looking green during periods of little or no rainfall.

▲ Tourist trekking in the Annapurna Mountains in Nepal is now very popular, and visitors are encouraged to act responsibly to conserve the environment for future visitors and local people.

Forest Loss

Tourist demands for wood are causing serious loss of forests in some poor countries, such as Nepal, one of the world's least developed nations. Nepalis are dependent on wood for nearly 80 percent of the energy they need for heating and cooking. Forests produce food, such as leaves to feed their animals and bamboo to make household items like baskets. Trekking tourism is now very popular and provides valuable money for the country and for local communities. However, a small tourist lodge uses around 10 times as much wood as a local household. Wood is used for heating, cooking, and to build lodges. Two and a half acres (1 ha) of rhododendron forest a year was estimated to be cut, to provide for the needs of trekkers visiting one small village along a popular trekking route in the Annapurna region. Women and children, who have the job of collecting wood, are having to walk increasing distances to find it. The current amount of wood used for tourism cannot be maintained, and already a shortage of wood is causing increasing hardship for local people, some of whom do not benefit from tourism.

Now, in the most popular trekking areas, notably the Annapurna Conservation Area, efforts are being made to ease the problem. Alternatives to wood for energy, such as solar power and small hydro projects that use the energy from fast-flowing Himalayan streams, have been provided in many villages. Tourists are encouraged not to make open fires, but to wear more clothing instead and to avoid hot showers in lodges that are burning wood.

Banaue Rice Terraces

The Banaue rice terraces are 2,000 years old and were cut, largely by hand, into the mountains of Ifugao in the Philippines. They cover 4,000 square miles (10,360 sq km) of mountainside and are fed by an ancient watering system from forests above the terraces. The terraces are sometimes called the world's eighth wonder and are a highly popular tourist site, but tourism is threatening their future.

The native Ifugao people who work the rice terraces traditionally have small wooded areas managed by families, which they use for basic needs such as firewood, medicine, and housing materials. Part of their custom is to carefully select a special tree cut for a particular purpose. Now, more kinds of trees are being cut to supply tourists with woodcarvings and handicrafts. The woodcarving industry has become very commercial, and so many trees are being used that the Banaue terraces are now threatened by erosion.

Have Your Say

Tourists visiting an area often use up valuable resources, such as water, that are vital for the lives of local people.

- Tourists pay a large amount of money to go on vacation—should they have to worry about consuming local resources?
- Should tourists be more careful when using natural resources such as water, especially as they use far more than local people?
- What ways might there be of limiting the impact of natural-resource consumption by tourists, without putting people off?

▼ The use of wood for creating tourist souvenirs has depleted this resource, so that the ancient terraces of Banaue, maintained by families who need wood for survival, have come under threat.

Environmental Impacts

Globalization in travel and tourism is having a dramatic effect on both local and global environments. On a personal and national level, people and countries all need to work hard to limit the negative effects and focus on the positive impacts that tourism can have on the environment.

Positive Impacts

Tourism can be a powerful force to protect and conserve environments. Increasingly, tourists are demanding high standards, such as scenic beauty and the improvement of urban areas to make them more attractive to visit, with the creation of traffic-free areas, for example. Tourism also provides the money needed to invest in clean-ups and other plans to improve the environment.

The last 50 years have seen a growth in protected areas, including national parks and wildlife reserves, which were originally designed to save threatened species and habitats. Today there are more than 5,000 protected areas worldwide, many of which are dependent on income from tourism, such as Kruger National Park in South Africa.

Beach tourism is among the most popular of all vacations. The tourist demands for clean beaches and coastal waters provide great encouragement to make improvements. The

Blue Flag is a well-respected, international award scheme, which guarantees to tourists that a beach or marina they are visiting is one of the best in the world. It is awarded to coastal vacation destinations that have achieved the highest quality in water, facilities, safety, and environment. The Blue Flag has led to the improvement of beaches around the world, and the number of beaches and marinas gaining Blue Flag status increases every year. More than 3,200 displayed the flag in 36 countries across Europe, South Africa, Morocco, New Zealand, Canada, and the Caribbean in 2006.

Negative Impacts

However, in many areas tourism is actually destroying what visitors come to find. Natural environments are being damaged and are disappearing. Much tourist development is both uncontrolled and badly planned. Beautiful landscapes have been damaged. Holiday resorts are sometimes poorly designed, overcrowded, and polluted.

Beaches are often maintained by the continual deposit of sand by ocean currents to replace the sand washed away by tides. Tourism is the main industry on Fuerteventura, one of the Canary Islands that is famous for its wonderful beaches. Today, widespread tourist development and sand mining have reduced

▲ The growth of skiing tourism in northern Europe has led to large numbers of tourists being introduced to remote environments that are easily damaged.

he amount of sand so much that beaches are much smaller than they were, and in some places they have completely disappeared.

Recreation, such as camping, picnicking, and hiking on sand dunes can lead to vegetation being worn away and eventually to erosion, for example, on the shore of Lake Ontario.

The wearing away of footpaths is a serious problem on popular walks in several parts of the uplands and coasts around the UK. In the Snowdonia National Park in north Wales, it is estimated that an average of 850 people per day walk to the summit of Snowdon, the highest mountain in Wales. Such large numbers erode the paths.

▼ Tourism has spread even to the frontier polar regions. It is fascinating to see such remote areas, but tourists can inadvertently hurt plant and animal life.

▲ The trash that tourists leave behind on beaches is not only unsightly, but is also damaging to the environment and wildlife.

Litter

In areas where many tourists gather, litter is often a major problem. It can spoil the environment around natural attractions such as waterfalls, beaches, famous buildings, scenic areas, and rivers. Carefully placed signs and garbage cans can help to raise visitors' awareness and reduce their dumping of trash. Bans on plastic bags and other plastic items are successful in some places—for example in the beautiful Nilgiri Hills, a major tourist area in south India, where an anti-plastic campaign was launched in 2001. The entire country of Bhutan is free of plastic bags; a ban has been enforced there since 1999.

Coastal Water Pollution

The Mediterranean is probably the world's most popular tourist destination, attracting one-third of the world's international tourists, but the industry has helped cause serious pollution in the sea. Overcrowded tourist buildings along the coast have caused erosion. Untreated sewage from hotels has polluted coastal waters. There are many laws that could protect the environment of the sea if they are enforced, but governments have still to show they will take the action needed.

Noise and Air Pollution

Noise pollution is sound that is harmful to humans or wildlife. It can be caused by tourist planes, cars, and buses, especially in areas that were previously quiet. This disturbs wildlife and spoils the peaceful atmosphere for both residents and tourists.

Exhaust fumes from too much traffic can cause serious air pollution and harm the environment. Tourists often rent cars or travel on tour buses when they arrive at their destination. Harmful gases from these vehicles add to air pollution.

Climate Change

Climate change is widely recognized as the Earth's most pressing environmental problem. It is affecting people around the world, in both MEDCs and LEDCs. Emissions of carbon dioxide into the atmosphere are

Focus on...
Coral Reefs

Coral reefs form one of the most beautiful and productive of the world's ecosystems, but also one of the most threatened. Tourists can harm reefs by diving, snorkelling, or boating, which can damage coral, and by the over-fishing and over-collecting of coral and life on the reef. Sediment from poorly managed tourist development smothers reefs. A number of organizations around the world are working to raise awareness and change behavior among both tourists and local tourist-industry workers. For example, the U.S.-based Coral Reef Alliance works globally to give advice on how to protect coral reefs while enjoying activities around them.

a major cause. Air travel is the fastest-growing source of carbon dioxide emissions. The amount of the gas produced by air travel doubled between 1990 and 2004. It accounts for less than five percent of world emissions of carbon dioxide, compared to 18 percent emitted from road traffic and 25 percent from homes. However, the share from air travel is rising. Tourism accounts for 60 percent of all air travel. Increasingly, tourists are going on vacation by plane, as flights are becoming cheaper and more convenient. Flying abroad for short vacations is now popular in many MEDCs.

▼ Healthy coral reefs like this one support thriving tourism industries and in some places, bring in billions of tourist dollars.

Have Your Say

Climate change is a major global threat to people and environments, and by going on vacation by air, we are making the problem worse because of the polluting gases produced by planes.

- When we go on vacation, should we stop flying altogether, or take fewer, longer vacations to help reduce carbon dioxide emissions?
- As tourism is important in many LEDCs, some of which have no other way to earn money, should we keep flying, to ensure their tourism industries are safe?
- Should we find other ways of cutting the amount of carbon dioxide we emit, such as using less energy for heating and lighting?

▲ Wetlands valuable for wildlife, such as those in Coto Donana in Spain, continue to be threatened by tourism. Building new resorts here is contributing to the lower water levels threatening the wetland's existence.

Dangers to Wildlife

Tourists can easily disturb wildlife, frightening the animals and preventing them from feeding or looking after their young properly. A recent study of nesting giant petrels in Antarctica found the birds' heartbeats rapidly increased when tourists came too close and recommended they stay at least 5 yards (50 m) away.

Road traffic often kills wildlife and can be especially dangerous if roads run through protected areas. An access road for tourists in Thailand's Khao-Yai National Park is too wide for the park's resident gibbons to cross, limiting their range.

Every year, tourists try to return home with souvenirs of endangered wildlife, or with products made from them, such as handbags from cobra skins, corals, tortoiseshells, and orchids. This is illegal, but often tourists simply do not realize that by buying wildlife souvenirs, they may be reducing the numbers of an endangered animal or plant. Many airports now display advice on the law about carrying wildlife and wildlife products.

Careless divers and their boats have seriously damaged some coral reefs by dragging boat anchors over reefs, trampling on the coral, and removing coral pieces for souvenirs.

▲ The mountain gorilla is highly endangered. Tourists can pay to see mountain gorilla groups in Rwanda. Mountain gorilla tourism is an important source of money for the country.

Have Your Say

Environmental issues have both helped and hindered the tourism industry in many countries.

- Is it right to expect tourists to pay more for "eco-friendly" vacations?
- How might awareness be heightened of the negative impacts of tourists buying souvenirs that have been made from illegal substances such as ivory?
- Should foreign governments be investing in conservation projects because they can benefit everyone, or is it the responsibility of local people to take care of their own environment?

A Positive Force for Conservation

If handled carefully, wildlife tourism can really benefit conservation. Tourist interest and awareness can be raised. The money paid by tourists can be used to help animals and to benefit local communities, encouraging people to protect wildlife and the places where they live.

The Azores islands in the Atlantic used to be one of the main centers of whale hunting until it was banned in the 1980s. Now, whale watching has taken its place, and the Azores have become one of the best places in the world to see dolphins and whales.

The Kinabatagan River runs through tropical rainforest threatened by felling for oil-palm plantations. Boat trips through the forest run by local people are very popular, letting tourists see rare mammals, such as orangutans and proboscis monkeys, at close range without disturbing them. The trips provide much-needed cash for local villagers and give them reason to protect the forests.

Focus on...
Earthwatch

Earthwatch is an international organization that enables volunteers to help conservation directly by joining an expedition. Supporters can work with an international team of volunteers at exciting and remote destinations around the world, alongside biologists studying wildlife and important environment issues. Watching elephant behavior in the Red Volta River Valley in Vietnam and protecting sea-turtle hatchlings on the beaches of Costa Rica are just two of the projects on the frontline of conservation.

Responsible Travel

The globalization of travel and tourism has placed great stress on cultures, communities, environments, and wildlife. It is not tourism itself that is damaging, but unmanaged and badly managed tourism. Those who support sustainable tourism are aware of these dangers and try to protect their favorite destinations and reduce the effects on local people.

Sustainable Tourism

Sustainable tourism meets the needs of tourists and the places they visit at the present time, while protecting and improving opportunities for the future. The rights of local people are respected. Local communities have an equal share in the economic benefits of tourism. Hotels and restaurants are owned and run by local people, for example. They help decide about tourist developments where they live and work. Sustainable tourism is carried out so that wildlife and the environment are undamaged, and each has the opportunity for renewal.

Some countries have special national plans to make sure the challenges of making tourism sustainable are overcome. One of the best examples is in Bhutan, where the government recognizes the need to develop the industry sustainably. Bhutan is a country about the size of Switzerland in the eastern Himalayas, with spectacular mountain scenery. It is largely unspoiled by development. Tourism is

▲ These are tour buses outside a hotel in Bhutan. Meeting and dealing with visitors has helped to make Bhutanese proud of their country's culture and environment.

controlled by limiting the number of visitors to the country each year and by taking a very cautious approach to any tourism development. The Bhutanese government charges each tourist a high daily fee of $200, and this money is reinvested in the country.

Island Tourism

Small island states, in particular, have adopted sustainable tourism plans. Tourism is often vital to these nations, many of which are too small to support large industry, but attract foreign tourists—especially islands with tropical climates. A few years ago, the government of Fiji recognized the country was not benefiting economically from tourism as much as it should. More than 60 percent of the money coming into Fiji from tourism was

▲ Fiji now operates a sustainable tourism program that has helped conserve its environment and improve the economy.

going back to tourists' own countries. Tourism development was also causing serious damage to some parts of the island's environment. As a result, in 2003, the government took action to follow the recommendations of a tourism development plan to try and make the industry sustainable.

Will sustainable tourism meet the challenge of protecting the world's last great places and their local native peoples while providing unique experiences for travelers? It will take the combined efforts of tourists, local communities, governments and businesses of visited countries, conservationists, and tour operators to make sure this happens.

Carbon Offsetting

As trees absorb carbon dioxide in their living processes, planting trees can help compensate for carbon dioxide emitted during air travel. This is known as carbon offsetting. Some airlines and travel companies are promoting projects where travelers pay an extra sum to plant trees that compensate for the carbon emissions caused by their flight. However, many environmentalists believe that while people should be encouraged to take steps to reduce their carbon dioxide emissions, it is both wrong and dangerous to imagine that paying a few dollars towards an offset project means that we can carry on polluting at the rates we are at the moment.

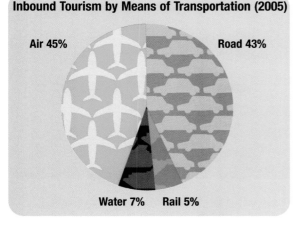

Inbound Tourism by Means of Transportation (2005)

Air 45%　　　　Road 43%

Water 7%　　Rail 5%

Focus on...
The Green Globe

The "Green Globe" is the leading worldwide set of standards formed to help create sustainable travel and tourism. It includes two kinds of standards, one for tour operators and the other for tourist destinations. Green Globe aims to increase awareness of the effects of tourism on native people and the environment. Other benefits are lower energy costs and improved efficiency. All areas of tourism are covered, including cities, hotels, cruise ships, transport action, and attractions.

Ecotourism

Ecotourism means conserving the environment and improving the welfare of local people when visiting natural areas. If managed properly, ecotourism can educate visitors, help promote natural environments, and benefit local people and local economies. Usually, ecotourism vacations focus on wilderness adventures, looking for wildlife, enjoying local culture and finding new, environmentally friendly ways of living on the planet. For some countries, including Costa Rica, Ecuador, and Kenya, ecotourism is a valuable attraction and an important national money-earner.

Ecotourism is growing much faster than the rest of the tourism industry, but in practice the term "ecotourism" is widely misunderstood. It is often just used to sell vacations that are related to nature. Staying in a hotel placed in a wild natural environment may be described by a travel agent as ecotourism, but building and running the hotel might be damaging the surrounding ecosystem. Companies may use an "eco" label without providing benefits to local people, cultures, or environments. This is often known as "greenwashing."

One problem is that some of the places visited by ecotourists are extremely sensitive and can be harmed even by careful tourists. The Amazonian rainforest and bird-breeding colonies in Antarctica are examples of this.

▲ Tourists are going further afield. This riverboat takes ecotourists up the River Negro, a tributary of the Amazon. They get to meet indigenous people and hear about their fight for land and justice in the deep interior of the Amazon rainforest.

Focus on...
Cycling in the U.S.

A cycling vacation is fun, keeps you fit, enables you to explore at your own pace, and to experience real ecotourism vacation. The Adventure Cycling Association has linked low-traffic roads and trails through some of the nation's most scenic and historic country to produce the National Bicycle Route Network. This now covers a vast distance of 36,180 miles (58,266 km). Route maps that show services, such as restaurants, campgrounds, and hotels are available. It's even possible to cycle right across America on the Trans-America Bicycle Trail, which takes you past lush forests, high deserts, mountain passes, snow-capped peaks, fertile farmlands, rolling hills, and ocean coasts.

How to Avoid Greenwashing

The best way of finding out if a vacation is true ecotourism and not a greenwash is to check if it is certified. Although there is no global program, there are programs in many parts of the world that certify vacations as true ecotourism. Examples include the Nature and Ecotourism Accreditation Program in Australia, Blue Flag and Protected Area Network in Europe, Sustainable Tourism in Costa Rica, and Smart Voyager in the Galapagos islands.

▲ Ecotourism is the second-largest source of income in Costa Rica. This is a "sky walk" in the Monteverde Biological Reserve.

True ecotourism includes programs that try to reduce the negative effects of traditional tourism on the environment and improve the culture of local people. Recycling waste materials, the efficient use of energy, reusing water, and creating new opportunities for local people to earn money are all involved.

However, the air travel needed to reach many tourist destinations is not included in judging the environmental impacts of a vacation in eco-certification programs. Some people believe we cannot have a sustainable or ecotourism vacation if we fly abroad, because of the serious problem of polluting gases from planes. There are many vacations that can be enjoyed at home that avoid this problem, and the starting points can be reached by road or rail—cycling, kayaking, walking, mountain climbing, and wildlife watching, for instance.

▲ These pagodas in Myanmar are erected as shrines and have a great cultural significance for local people. They have become some of the area's greatest tourist attractions, but it is important to show respect for their religious importance when visiting.

Responsible Tourism

Even if we are not able to have a truly sustainable or ecotourism vacation if we fly abroad, we can still make sure that we travel responsibly. Responsible tourism is about bringing visitors closer to local cultures and environments by involving local people in tourism. It is about doing this in a fair way that respects and benefits local communities. It conserves environments, too. Efforts are now underway within many native communities to create new guidelines and controls to promote responsible tourism. As visitors are gaining more from this kind of vacation, responsible tourism is becoming more popular among people from different countries.

Machu Picchu

Machu Picchu, an Inca fortress in the Andes mountains of Peru, is one of the world's best-known ancient monuments. Although the number of people on the trail every day is limited to help protect Machu Picchu, a bridge was opened in 2007 to provide new access by road. This will make controlling tourist numbers impossible.

Tourism is also threatening the links between the Inca's descendants and their sacred site. Until a few years ago, they were not able to take part in deciding management of the fortress. Ancient burial sites have been spoiled and human remains removed and put on display for tourists. However, recently the indigenous peoples have been actively involved in working to preserve their spiritual and cultural way of life through a non-governmental organization (NGO) called Yashay Wasi. In 2006, the Yashay Wasi urged the United Nations to consult with native communities on the best way to

▲ As many as half a million people every year visit Machu Picchu, and this is damaging the site. The indigenous people are now looking for ways to protect their heritage.

protect and promote World Heritage sacred sites. The Yashay Wasi has produced a list of guidelines of conduct for tourists, to help them behave responsibly when visiting sacred sites in Peru.

Community-Based Tourism Initiatives

Many local communities are aware of the power of responsible tourism in helping local economic development. Based in areas of outstanding natural heritage, they take on the challenge of setting up community-based tourism projects, usually with the help of local and/or international NGOs.

Conservation International, a U.S.-based NGO, and Responsible Travel are promoting community-based vacations. For example, in San José, Guatemala, community association and homestay projects provide

the opportunity to learn about the native Itzá culture and Spanish language. In Kyrgyzstan, it is possible to stay with a family or live the nomadic life, experiencing local traditions. Visitors can taste national dishes, see how goats are milked, and make souvenirs, for example. These programs encourage respect for, and understanding of, the culture.

Focus on...
Rainforest Alliance

The Rainforest Alliance, with offices in New York City, around the U.S., and worldwide, works with people whose livelihoods depend on the land, helping them transform the way they grow food, harvest wood, and host travelers. It sets standards for sustainability that conserve wildlife and promote the well-being of workers and their communities.

Obstacles to Responsible Tourism

A recent study of brochures of U.S. tour operators offering vacations in Kenya revealed they did not educate tourists on culturally responsible behavior. This is true of many tour operators in MEDCs.

Mass-marketed package tours combine flights, transfers, and accommodations and are often cheap. They give value for money, sunshine, and the chance to relax in a safe environment, which is what many people want. More than 10 million of these vacations are sold every year around the world. However, tourists in large numbers often damage cultures and environments, and can cause serious problems for thriving local communities.

Having a Responsible Vacation

We can all make a difference. Thinking about what effect your vacation will have on the community you visit is the key. Considering how your money can bring the greatest benefits to the community is important, too. Taking a responsible approach to your vacation should help you enjoy it more, by bringing you closer to local cultures.

▼ Local people should always be treated with respect. If you wish to photograph them, ask permission first.

- Before you travel, read up on local cultures and learn a few words of the local language. Do not be afraid of trying out these words—locals will probably appreciate the effort you have made.
- Ask your tour operator for tips for responsible travel in your destination.
- Find out if there are useful gifts you could pack for your hosts, local people, or schools.
- Ask your tour operator if there are local conservation or social projects you could visit on your trip, and if or how you could help support them.
- Try to use a tour operator from the host country, which will help support the local economy.
- Respect local cultures, traditions, and holy places.
- Remember that local people may have different ways of thinking and concepts of time than you—this just makes them different, not wrong.
- Wear clothing that locals consider to be appropriate.
- Ask before taking pictures of people and respect their wishes.
- Don't give anything to children, even something as small as a pencil, as this encourages begging. Donate to a school or health center instead.
- Be fair over costs. If you haggle for the lowest price, your bargain may be at the seller's expense.
- Talk to local people and ask questions. Do not assume that the western way is right or best.
- If you are traveling with a tour operator, ask to see their written policy for responsible travel. If it is not written down, they are not accountable and are probably not taking it seriously.

▲ When traveling, always be aware of local customs and beliefs and follow respectful dress codes and behavior.

Eyewitness

"Much of the travel media, rather like the travel industry, don't think it their business to uncover any worries about how communities might suffer in the name of tourism. They are bored with the issues. For some editors, there is simply too much pressure to be successful in selling vacations. Today, upbeat is good."
Travel journalist and lecturer in tourism

The Great Debate

Tourism is the world's largest industry and one of the fastest growing. It is vital to many nations' economies and is especially important to developing nations, which have few natural resources. But there are disadvantages as well.

Advantages include:

- Tourism helps improve the economy in many LEDCs, by providing jobs and by bringing in foreign money for goods and services sold.

- Understanding, friendship, and respect for other cultures can develop between visitors and hosts.

- Tourism can encourage pride in and preservation of local and national traditions, arts and crafts, and sites.

- Carefully managed wildlife tourism can benefit conservation efforts as well as local communities.

Disadvantages include:

- A large percentage of money spent by tourists often does not go to the local economy, but to foreign travel companies.

- Countries may become too dependent on tourism dollars, so they are bady affected if war or natural disasters keep people away.

- Traditional ceremonies and rituals performed for tourists begin to lose meaning.

- Tourists use up resources, such as energy and water, much more quickly than local people.

Facts and Figures

World's Top Tourist Destinations (2005)

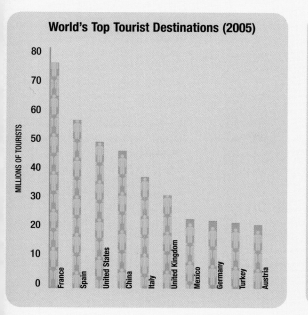

MILLIONS OF TOURISTS

France, Spain, United States, China, Italy, United Kingdom, Mexico, Germany, Turkey, Austria

Predicted Growth in International Tourist Spending

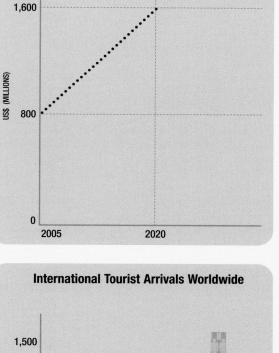

US$ (MILLIONS)

1,600

800

0

2005   2020

Tourism Spending (2005)

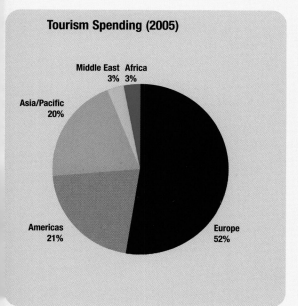

Middle East 3%   Africa 3%

Asia/Pacific 20%

Americas 21%

Europe 52%

International Tourist Arrivals Worldwide

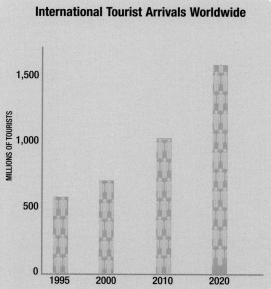

MILLIONS OF TOURISTS

1,500

1,000

500

0

1995   2000   2010   2020

43

Further Information

Books

Connolly, Sean. *Safeguarding the Environment.* Campaigns for Change. North Mankato, Minn.: Smart Apple Media, 2006.

Gifford, Clive. *Sustainable Development.* Face the Facts. Chicago: Raintree, 2004.

Hibbert, Adam. *Globalization.* Chicago: Raintree, 2005.

Lorimer, Kelly. *Code Green: Experiences of a Lifetime.* Melbourne: Lonely Planet, 2006.

Parks, Peggy J. *Ecotourism.* Farmington, Mich.: Kidhaven Press, 2006.

Stringer, John. *Energy.* Sustainable Futures. North Mankato, Minn.: Smart Apple Media, 2005.

Web Sites

www.unwto.org/index.php
The web site of the World Tourism Organization, with up-to-date statistics and information on tourism.

www.rainforest-alliance.org
The Rainforest Alliance works with people whose livelihoods depend on the land, helping them transform the way they grow food, harvest wood, and host travelers.

www.iipt.org
The International Institute for Peace through Tourism (IIPT) promotes tourism projects which help international understanding and cooperation, an improved quality of environment, and the preservation of heritage.

www.sustainabletravelinternational.org/
Sustainable Travel International (STI) promotes sustainable development and responsible travel.

www.ecotourism.org
The International Ecotourism Society (TIES) promotes responsible travel to natural areas that conserves the environment and improves the well-being of local people.

www.lonelyplanet.com/responsibletravel/
The responsible tourism section of the Lonely Planet travel guide website offers plenty of top tips for your next vacation.

Teaching Resources

www.ssrc.org/sept11/essays/teaching_resource/tr_globalization.htm
The Social Science Research Council provides essays, lesson plans, and teaching guides on topics such as globalization and terrorism.

www.pbs.org/americanfieldguide/teachers/natl_parks/natl_parks_sum.html
PBS provides teacher resources and lesson plans for its Ecotourism in National Parks and Wilderness unit.

www.prb.org/Educators/LessonPlans/2001/Ecotourism.aspx
A project-based lesson plan to help students understand the benefits of ecotourism.

www.eduweb.com/amazon.html
This site teaches the geography of the Amazon Rain Forest and has an interactive game in which students can run their own ecotourism company.

Glossary

archeological site a place in which evidence of past human activity is preserved.

citizen a person living in a country or city.

climate change the rise in global temperatures that is causing changes in the climate, including heavy rains and violent storms. Climate change takes place naturally, but human activities are increasing its rate. The burning of fuels that interfere with the natural balance of gases in the atmosphere is largely to blame.

commercial done to make money.

community groups of people in a particular area who live and work together.

conservation the active management of the Earth's natural resources and the environment to ensure their quality is maintained and that they are wisely used.

coral reefs features found in the sea formed from large numbers of coral polyps—tiny animals with a hard skeleton. They are one of the most productive and spectacular ecosystems.

deforestation the cutting down or destruction of forests.

development actions by humans that change the natural landscape, including the building of houses, roads and factories.

economy the supply of money gained by a community or country from goods and services.

ecosystem all the plants and animals in an area, along with their environment.

environment of a living entity, this consists of all the things (biological, chemical, and physical) that affect it.

erosion the process of being worn away, for example by wind or water.

exploitation the process of being used to disadvantage.

foreign-exchange earnings money that a country earns by selling things.

globalization the growth of something on a worldwide scale.

habitat the place where a plant or animal lives.

heritage practices that are handed down from the past by tradition.

indigenous local and native.

less economically developed country (LEDC) one of the poorer countries of the world. LEDCs include all of Africa, Asia (except for Japan), Latin America and the Caribbean, and Melanesia, Micronesia, and Polynesia.

more economically developed country (MEDC) one of the richer countries of the world. MEDCs include all of Europe, North America, Australia, New Zealand, and Japan.

native someone who comes from a particular area.

over-fishing taking too many fish from the sea so that stocks reduce.

pollution the presence of high levels of harmful substances in the environment, often as a result of human activity.

population a group of living things of the same species that inhabit a particular area.

protected area an area set aside to protect wildlife and their habitats.

recycling the process by which materials are collected and used again as "raw" materials to make new products.

renewable energy energy that is generated from sources that can be replaced or renewed; renewable resources include wind and sun.

resource a stock or supply of materials or other useful or valuable things. Natural resources include wood, water, oil, and minerals.

sediment matter that settles to the bottom of a liquid. Sediments are found on the seabed.

solar power energy that comes from the sun.

species a particular type of animal or other living creature.

sustainable able to continue to support itself indefinitely

tropical rainforest forest that grows in an area that is very hot and with high rainfall all year. It supports a higher number of different kinds of plants and animals than any other ecosystem.

wetlands lands made up of marshes or swamps.

Index